GREAT RIVER REVIEW

GREAT RIVER REVIEW

Number 25

Fiction Editor
    Pamela Davies

Poetry Editor
    Orval Lund, Jr.

Managing Editor
    Monica Drealan DeGrazia

Consulting Editor
    Emilio DeGrazia

Great River Review is published twice yearly by Great River Review, Inc., a non-profit corporation. Unsolicited manuscripts of poetry, fiction, essays and reviews are welcome but must be accompanied by a self-addressed, stamped envelope. All manuscripts, queries, subscriptions and correspondence should be sent to:

>Great River Review
>211 West 7th Street
>Winona, MN 55987

This issue of *Great River Review* is made possible in part by a Southeastern Minnesota Arts Council McKnight Community Arts Education Partnership Grant funded by the McKnight Foundation and Winona State University. We are grateful.

The cover is from a woodcut by* **Julia Crozier.

>ISBN 1-884102-02-6
>©1995 by Great River Review, Inc.
>All Rights Reserved
>Printed in the United States of America

CONTENTS

Prose
- Mitch Grabois — *The Depth of the Ducks* — 1

Featured Poet
- John Reinhard — 14

Prose
- Scott W. Wrobel — *For Jake's Sake* — 33

Poetry
- Deborah Cummins — *Nothing's Safe* — 39
- *One Million Rwandan...* — 41
- Robert Edwards — *The Mud Lake, Minnesota...* — 42
- *My Uncle, Willis* — 44
- Tom Hansen — *Those Long Days...* — 47
- L. L. Harper — *Hollis* — 48
- *Their Fathers Were Beautiful* — 49
- Jeanne Lyon — *Looking for a Heart* — 50
- Jim Murphy — *October Sunbath...* — 52
- Howard Nelson — *The Buck* — 53
- *Eating Eggs* — 55
- Linda Goodman Robiner — *High School Sex* — 56
- *Pretzels in Bed* — 57
- Matthew Spireng — *Cabbage Whites* — 58

Prose
- Marianne Barnett — *Mutations* — 59

Featured Poet
- *Florence Dacey* — 68

Prose
- Ellen Hawley — *At Jesus' Feet* — 83

Contributors' Notes — 90

THE DEPTH OF THE DUCKS

Mitch Grabois

1

My wife of forty years rests peacefully in her grave. Her spirit has long departed, lifting like fog over rice fields. Sometimes I try to fight and bicker with her, but she is indifferent.

My son has been marred by her absence, as well as by (in his estimation) my presence. His history holds him down. He would like to spring away, a diver springing from the top of a cliff into the thrashing waters below. I saw this sporting event on the TV in the Standing Buddha Saloon, in the village.

My son, walking by the street, looked in and caught me watching. He barked, "Hah! You are a modern man after all, watching *Wide World of Sports*! Now we will see how quick you are to chastise me!"

For months afterward, in the Standing Buddha, I sneaked peeks at the screen, feeling like a dog with its tail between its legs.

The athleticism of the sports figures mesmerizes me. The images of gymnasts and figure skaters, skiers and swimmers, cascade down on me like feathers from an exploded pillow.

I watch oiled men and women make muscles, their bodies like bunkers. I have determined from the British in the Standing Buddha that only since the War have the Invaders grown like this. My simultaneous attraction, repulsion, and fear make my stomach churn. In the empty lot behind the Standing Buddha, I hunch over and my stomach clenches like a fist. Beer shoots from my nostrils. My sinuses have pain like dry sticks cracking.

My son says, "You are getting more foolish each year. You are becoming your own grandfather."

I do not say the obvious, that he is becoming his own father, though I was never as brash as he. My rage is an animal I keep on a strong leash. If I could become my grandfather in my grandfather's time I would gladly do so. He was deaf, and early in life he'd had a revelation that silence is compassion, so he was always a happy man. Little disturbed him, and he died, mercifully, before the Invaders came.

The red Invader (I think of her as "The Red One") is unquiet in her grave. Throughout the years she has heaved about down there, and I have often awakened, tossing and turning, to realize we are still fighting.

But in the morning the house has always been peaceful. The sod of the walls absorbs my nightmares and composts them to silence. I light the fire and put on water for tea. We have many earthen jars stuffed with tea leaves.

When he was younger, my son and I had many battles over Coca Cola. He wanted it badly. Then, when he was almost overwhelmed by the steadfastness of my refusal, he would switch to Pepsi Cola, and we would begin anew. I would say, "My son, you cannot beat me. The Invaders came and came, and they could not beat us. I will not give you money for their drinks."

"But they are soft drinks," my son would say, as if that invested them with virtue. Yet he could see he had confused me.

I remember once secretly pouring Pepsi over my palm. I was that kind of tactile fellow. It was prickly, foamy, sticky, not soft. I remember once shouting at him, "IT IS NOT SOFT!!!" I remember my wife's strange look, asking, "What are you trying to prove? You have accomplished all that could be accomplished."

Later, years after her death, walking on the dirt road from the village to my home, I found myself with a strong, impossible urge to bring her to the Standing Buddha, to show her, on the TV, the new generation of Invaders, making muscles, their bodies like bunkers.

***

I ask my son what he thinks of these bodies. We are in our home; the walls are breathing silence. He is like me, small and slight. He peers at me as if I am trying to get something out of him, or get something over on him. But then he relaxes. The question has made him turn inward. The meditative state fits him awkwardly, yet I feel we are, for the moment, closer.

He gets up from his chair and leaves the room. I hear him in the hallway, opening his bedroom door. He returns and hands me a magazine. Across the top in big blue letters it reads, *Body Builder Magazine*. I open it with the feeling of uncooked rice pouring through my fingers.

My son has cut the heads from his final secondary school pictures, now three years old, and pasted them to the bodies of these "body builders." Not just the males, but the females as well. The incongruity is so sharp and sudden that I cannot keep from laughing.

Yet, even in my own ears, my laughter sounds harsh. That was not my intention. My son flushes red, then purple. I do not understand what is happening, but I know I have betrayed him, and that I have damaged our relationship in a way that may take a long time to heal.

He grabs the magazine and stalks off. I feel that if he were able to launch himself through the walls, he would do so. I leave the house by its back door and walk straight into an unplanted field. Muscovy ducks gather around me, snaking their heads. I turn around and look at my home, its red roof overhanging its sod walls. In the background are mountains, but directly around the house is flat farmland.

I sense my son in the house watching me through a window. I cannot see him but feel he is there, spying. I see myself as he sees me, slightly hunched, wearing coarse blue trousers and a coarse brown work shirt which hang from my body, an older man in a field surrounded by fat, black and white, masked ducks. Actually, these ducks are not really ducks, I'm told by the English in the Standing Buddha, but a type of goose.

In the Standing Buddha have been many English. They have, they tell me, a post-colonial urge to insert themselves in tropical places distant from England. After much time spent with them, I think I understand, and it does not threaten me. I like to sit with them at the big round table they call their "Outpost." One young woman, a blonde with bright blue eyes, says she is studying at the University to be a podiatrist. I ask her what is a podiatrist.

"A foot doctor," she says.

An Englishman, who's been drinking heavily, says, "I think that would be absolutely awful, examining people's smelly feet, day after day, asking them to take off their shoes, seeing their grubby socks, smelling that putrid cooped-up foot odor."

"There is much wisdom in feet," I say, more to please the young woman than because it is something I believe. Even as I say it, I remember feet I have seen. The beer the Englishmen have bought me carries a virtual flood of feet. I remember my wife's feet, small and delicate. Even as she aged her feet seemed not to, though her hands grew to look old and rough. I remember the feet of her brother, the bones standing out in ridges. I see the overburdened knees and feet of the very fat, and feel a wave of pity for what our bodies are subjected to. I remember the feet of "The Red One," the red Invader. I remember thinking her body looked as if it had been boiled, and it was freckled all over with red freckles, as if sprinkled with paprika. Even her feet were dusted with red, white feet with unusually high arches, like bridges over streams.

"There's a lot of money in feet," says the podiatry student, but she sounds unconvinced.

In my mind's eye I see a foot stuffed with coins, its skin bumpy with their edges. It takes me a moment to realize she means she would be paid much money for doctoring feet. "The English must have bad feet," I say.

This creates an uproar among the group. "Maybe during the Industrial Age," one protests, "when we stood for fourteen hours laboring in front of machines. But not now."

"I'd be willing to bet," says another, "that the English have the most sallow and characterless feet in the world. And flat. I'd wager we have more flat feet per capita than any other nation on Earth."

"Actually," says the podiatry student, "English feet are very well supported."

When they have exhausted the topic of feet, they begin discussing the trials and tribulations of the British royal family. I have trouble keeping all the characters straight and after a while I rise unsteadily, belch, and move away from the table.

I feel stiff and old and realize my own feet hurt. I wonder if Clara, the podiatry student, would look at them, though I have no money to give her. I would like her to take my feet in her strong, young hands and examine them, as if they were fish—coy, with bulging eyes—netted from a pond. Then she would gently slide them back into the water.

***

I walked back along the old dirt trail, purposely shoeless, my shoes in my back pockets, hanging like a dog's ears. This blonde

Clara had reminded me of "The Red One." I sensed the same ferocity in her, though it was largely hidden. I imagined her with a pearl handled knife, plunging it through a man's foot into a hardwood floor. Where I had gotten this image I could not say. I was convinced that, in any important way, none of the English males at the Standing Buddha would be a match for Clara. I would not be surprised if she were trained in the martial arts. In my mind's eye, I could see her chopping patients' feet with the edge of her hand. My imagination, I realize, had a limited range, and many of my thoughts are tied to those days of the War of the Invaders.

There were no airplanes in that war, and few guns. It was a strangely silent war, fought primarily hand-to-hand. The cries and grunts of the fighting pierced the silence of the countryside.

At first only our men fought, but later our women also. Their women, stripped of demands for nurturing, had become so fierce. "The Red One" had come screaming at me, like a figure from mythology. She knocked me down, but when I got up I punched her in the solar plexus and knocked the wind out of her. We fought. She was bigger and heavier, but I was young, toughened by farm work, defending my land. My sting was like a scorpion's. Finally I broke her neck.

***

Lying dead, she seemed even larger than when she'd been alive. I felt like a giant killer from a fairy tale. I thought: it was their bulk which made these Invaders so sure of triumph. Yet throughout our country, small slim people like myself stood in awe of our efficacy in administering death. Previously all I'd ever killed were fowl. I'd plunged their dead bodies into a cauldron of boiling water and plucked their feathers from them.

Now I pulled the clothes from this woman I'd killed, who'd flown down screaming a war cry, her red hair flying. Under her uniform she was wearing black underwear. I released the clasp of her brassiere. Her breasts were large and when I removed the brassiere they spilled out with a sensual indolence. Death had transformed her from an animal to a woman, but a kind of woman I had never seen. My own wife was small and angular, like myself, dark and spare.

I removed her black underpants. Her pubic hair was as red as the hair on her head. It shocked me. Each of the bright red spots which freckled her body were erotic reiterations. Even in death she frightened me. I half expected her to spring to life, and attack me again, in her nakedness. How would I battle her then?

I felt angry at her, angry at the Invaders, waging this war. But my anger subsided and I felt tenderness toward this woman I had killed. I felt it was right she be undraped to the countryside she had sought to conquer. Instead of domination, she had attained intimacy.

Finally her nakedness aroused me. Her thigh was warm to my touch. I fantasized spreading her thighs and mounting her—there was nothing to stop me. Her warm flesh would well up to surround me as I sank into her. I would clutch her ample buttocks as fear, struggle, and death culminated in joy.

Then I shivered and pushed these thoughts from my mind. My impulse to necrophilia sickened me, though I felt no guilt about murdering her. She had been there to murder me. In fact, it was less a war than a flotilla of unleashed murderers. I was righteous, on my own property, in my own homeland.

I nervously scanned the area for other Invaders, but she, evidently, had been alone. This war was so strange—it was not only lacking in technology, but the Invaders seemed to have forgotten even such basics as strength in numbers. Were the Invaders so arrogant, or merely stupid?

I buried her in the forest beneath a tree, near a large limestone formation loaded with mosses and lichens. This kill, my first, had made me hypersensitive to color, to the white and red of my victim's body, and the blues, greens and greys of plant life. When the war was over, I thought, if I were still alive, I would become an artist.

However, when the war ended I forgot about color. I went back to raising ducks and raising my son, and playing my xedurox. The sound of my xedurox, with its many strings and resonating plates, never fails to mesmerize me.

***

During the past twenty years, in which I made the transition from being a young man to an old man, there have been many stories about the Invaders. Little children, who were not even alive then, run screaming in their games, "An Invader lives in the roots of that tree! An Invader lives in that hole!"

When the wind howls, the old people hear the shouts and screams of the Invaders. When a child is delinquent, it is said he has the spirit of the Invaders. Decomposing garbage is the stench of the Invaders. A tragedy is the return of the Invaders. So the Invaders are still with us. Having invaded us, though they were repelled, they will forever be a part of us, and we part of them.

In the country of the Invaders, in their elections, a candidate who, in their War, came to ravage us is considered to have an unblemished character. He will automatically receive many votes. One who did not enlist, has (to use our expression) "no milk, eggs, or blood"; he will have a stoney road convincing others he is worthy to lead.

They return now and say, "I fought here." It is difficult to know how to respond. We have heard about their nightmares. They do not know about ours.

We have heard about their madness. Some of them who overran our land sleep under bridges, like trolls. Or they live underground. By day they hold out their palms. They hold out signs: "Give me food." The English have told me about them.

***

The representative of the Invaders is over two meters tall, and thin as a board. His thin tie is a channel, a groove, down his middle. His suit is yellow. He chews tobacco and spits tobacco juice onto the dirt as he speaks with us. The children come around, wide-eyed, then run screaming, "Invader!" The bolder children swoop in like bats, swipe their hands across the man's pants legs, and scream. The boldest give his pants leg a yank as they streak by. He is annoyed, but tries not to show.

The Invader has a leather portfolio in which are hundreds of photographs. Some of them spill to the ground. He hands them around, wanting to know if we have ever seen these young Invader faces.

A teenage boy breaks in among us and says, in our language, "There is an Invader who lives in a cave by the river." The representative's interpreter translates. The representative raises his eyebrows, spits tobacco juice in the dirt, and asks, "Is this true?"

One of us says, "He lives under the river, but when he is full of water, he moves to the cave."

Another says, "The cave opens to a city of tunnels and caves. After the War of the Invaders, some Invaders went down there to live."

Then other voices join in. "They live without light and have all gone blind."

"They have reproduced—there are more of them now than there were before."

A teenager says, "If they ever come out, we will kill them." He is hushed by the older men.

Another says, "But if they do not come out, they will multiply until there is no room for them, and then the Earth will explode."

Another teenager, "...And their bodies will rain down on us."

"If one falls on a house, it will burst into flames!"

Out on the road, we pass the photographs from hand to hand. When they come to me, I shuffle through them as if they are playing cards.

There is silence save for the man's spitting. Portrait photography is uncommon in our land so we look at these photos carefully. We have a belief that spirit inhabits photography, so a photograph can be used for beneficence or evil.

In my hand is a photograph of "The Red One." I recognize her right away. This moment of convergence—me, she, her photograph—has been waiting to occur since I broke her neck and buried her in the woods.

2

Clara, the English podiatry student, is on the flagstone floor in front of our fireplace, kneading my feet in her hands. My son is nearby on the floor, doing pushups and sit-ups.

Clara hums intently as she rubs my feet. She has promised my son that when she returns to England she will have a Charles Atlas kit sent to him. He has shown her the copy of "Body Building Magazine." He does not seem to find any oddness in it. She looked at it solemnly. She has told him about genetics and steroids. I watched his face as she told him.

Since the representatives of the Invaders have been visiting, scouring the courntryside, my son and I seem to have grown closer together again. He seems afraid. I think he thinks that if the Invaders do not find what they are looking for they will do something unspeakable to us, for which we will have no defense. He cannot believe that our people actually repelled the Invaders. He looks at the Invaders and he looks at us and he cannot believe it. He sees they have the genetics and the steroids.

But he also doubts his doubts, because he wonders why there is a beautiful young English woman on the floor of our home, rubbing my feet. He wonders what the attraction is, and begins to wonder whether it is the attraction of the true history of our people, and the fact that, though he cannot see it, I was a mighty warrior. Clara sees it—she sees the man I was, young and virile. She know that self is still inside me, inside my feet! She can massage it to life.

(Bullshit! I cowered among my ducks, hoping no Invader would come to find me.)

Before the Invaders came and I administered death, I thought deep philosophical thoughts among my ducks. But after I had administered death I no longer had those thoughts. My meditations became flat and shallow, like water in a pan. Never again did I recover my depth, the depth of the ducks.

My wife knew the difference—sex was not the same. It was still enjoyable, but it had become more mechanical. I had lost my deeper connection to the planet. I had not expected this.

Philosophically I had been ready to become a killer, despite my cowardice. I always believed life demands death. Yet killing stripped me of my depth, made me flat. I think of this as I listen to the English in the Standing Buddha banter about the royal family.

I tell them about the photographs shown by the representative of the Invaders. The English are not sympathetic to the Invaders. They have critical comments to offer. They call the photographs *denial baseball cards* and *mug shots of the misplaced.*

Smiling, Clara says, "Don't listen to these blowhards. They are rabble, soccer stadium hooligans."

They feed me beer and I become angry. In the War of the Invaders, the Invaders brought photographers to record death, as if it were something treasured they wanted to preserve. They recorded their own atrocities, as if they were proud of them. They fixed them forever in silver emulsion.

I am no better, having fixed "The Red One" forever in my mind.

My memory of "The Red One" reminds me of the story of the

two Buddhist monks on a journey. They get to a shallow river where they find a courtesan wanting to cross but not wanting to get her fine dress wet. One of the monks carries her to the other side.

The second monk is horrified at his companion having done this. As they continue their travels he chews on it and chews on it until he can contain himself no longer. He bursts out, "How could you have carried that courtesan across the river, a woman of her kind?"

The first monk says, "Ah. I put her down at the edge of the river, but you have been carrying her ever since."

Clara says, "You must tell the representative about "The Red One."

***

Clara whispers to me, "The world is now in a Capricorn phase. Everywhere I've been I've had the same feeling—the world must be put in order before we can progress."

I ask, "What do you mean, *the world?*"

"All the unfinished business of the past."

We walk down dirt trails, holding hands. The moon is full. It has seemed more and more natural for myself, an isolated peasant, and Clara to be together. She and the English in the Standing Buddha have made me a different person.

We pass by a small group of Invaders wearing night vision gear. Since their lost war against us, they no longer trust flesh and blood. They must have machines to encounter the world. They examine us carefully as we go by. They believe there are discoveries they can make at night which they would be unable to make during the day.

"The only reason an Invader ever comes is to take something," I say. "It is not about putting the past in order—they are here to take away more magic, more energy, to further impoverish us."

"No. They are here because in their own land there are mothers and fathers and husbands and wives who have not been able to complete their grief. They are only here for information."

"There is no information which can complete grief. Grief is only completed by death. Life is suffering."

"Your government would not let them be here if they were going to harm you."

"Pah! Since the War, our government has drifted away, like smoke."

***

Today there are few English at the big round table in the Standing Buddha, and those who sit there are sodden and uncommunicative. One of them is sleeping hunched over in his chair, his "old school tie" immersed in a half-full pitcher of beer.

***

I say to Clara, "The Red One" is a cancer in my body. I am afraid to tell the Invaders about her."

"Why? You don't have to tell them you killed her, just that you know of the grave."

"I hope you are not insulted, but you remind me of her, big and loose-boned, indolent and ferocious."

"Why should I feel insulted?"

"I am comparing you to someone I murdered."

***

My son says, "I have been studying more deeply about the War. I've been reading about the helicopter gunships, the strafing, the napalm, the bombing, the burning of women and children alive in huts."

"I have heard those things," I reply, "but those are only the hallucinations of those who went mad. That was not the way the War was. The Invaders came in big wooden ships and dove into our waters, frightening us. They swam ashore and ran through the countryside, their clothes wet and torn. They attacked us with sticks and with their bare hands. Some of them had fishing knives. Some had baseball bats.

"They were objects of wonder, as we'd never seen baseball bats. I wrestled with an Invader for control of one. He'd crept up behind me and swung at my head. Luckily, at that moment, I stooped down to pick a mushroom. The bat whistled as it flew by, an inch from my ear. It was a beauty, made of aluminum, shiny like silver. It had the words *Louisville Slugger* pressed into its barrel. Many years later, I watched baseball for the first time on the TV in the Standing Buddha, and heard the clang of ball on bat...Why are you gaping at me, Clara?"

***

I dream of a ball bearing rolling down a steel track, surrounded by darkness. I awake covered in sweat, terrified. "The Red One" is struggling to move her petrified limbs. Somewhere in the land of the Invaders, someone may be remembering her.

I have the business card of the representative of the Invaders. It is not paper, but a kind of plastic so that it will not so easily disintegrate in the heat and humidity, so that it will remain, a lump lodged in my life, like a cancer. Two Buddhist monks walk away from a river. Finally one breaks down and cries, "How could you have carried that courtesan across the river?"

"If she is growing heavy, you may put her down," says the other.

"Your son knows you are not telling him the truth," Clara says. "And he showed me all his muscle magazines. He wants to be a freak, with hypertrophied muscles. Where do you think that impulse comes from?"

"Not to be insulting," I say, "but I wish my wife were here. For so many years we made decisions by pulling against each other—she was an unusual woman. We pulled against each other and somehow would find the middle path. Now I have to wade into the center, to make my own decision. I don't like it. And I feel my decisions are tentative, as if they are subject to revocation...."

"Would you like me to pull against you?"

I laugh. "Thank you Clara," I say, "but you are going to England to fix feet."

"Sometimes I feel I have made the stupidest of career decisions," she says. "I should never have listened to my advisor. Those tests they gave me were bogus. In England, the feet of the people are like slabs of bacon...Are you going to tell the representative about 'The Red One'?"

***

"I've decided to move to the city," my son says. I feel that the presence of the English in the Standing Buddha has affected him too and, though he has not said it, he is jealous of my relationship with Clara. After all she is much closer to his age than mine, and he does not get enough sex. "There are many good jobs in the city, and body building gyms," he says.

"Besides," I say, "You are tired of the hissing of all these ducks. You are tired of their smell, and their feathers. You loath seeing your father, the duck man. You want to distance yourself from ducks."

There is a knock on the door. "The representative of the Invaders is here," my son says.

We walk out to the woods. Clara holds my arm. My son follows. There is a small crew of men from the village, with shovels. I point to the site, beneath a tree, which has grown even taller through the years.

The men dig, but find nothing.

"Deeper," I say. "Deeper."

When the hole is impossibly deep, and the diggers are covered with sweat and dirt, the representative says. "There's nothing here. Are you sure this is the spot?"

I walk to a limestone outcropping, and stare at its familiar blooms of lichen and mosses. I look back to the deep hole, with the dirt piled up around it. I am confused and uncertain of something which I could not have been more certain about. I say, "Perhaps here."

When we are finally through, the area is waffled with holes. The persistence of the representative has equalled my uncertainty and confusion. I sink against Clara.

My son says. "More lies," contempt in his voice. "Did you kill *anyone* during the War?" he says.

John Reinhard

photo by Leigh Marthe

John Reinhard
FEATURED POET

JOHN REINHARD is the author of two collections of poems, *Burning the Prairie* (1988) and *On the Road to Patsy Cline* (due early 1996), both winners of the Minnesota Voices Project competition sponsored by New Rivers Press. He was born in Sault Ste. Marie, Michigan, in 1953, earned degrees from Eastern Michigan University, and worked on his MFA at the University of Michigan where he won a Hopwood Award and Cowden Fellowship. Teaching jobs at the University of Minnesota-Morris and Winona State University brought him to Minnesota and have kept him here. A former Loft-McKnight Award winner for poetry, he now lives in St. Paul and does any hack work he can find while also teaching at the Loft.

Of the poems below, "Great Uncle Norvell Fast Is Dead" and "Not Letting Go of Lauren Bacall" are from *Burning the Prairie*; the remainder will be published in *On the Road to Patsy Cline*.

Not Letting Go of Lauren Bacall

My grandfather loved her. Maybe
it was the voice like bourbon, the walk
that tightened up your trousers. Maybe
he saw himself as Bogart, the hat
always low on the forehead and the eyes
in shadow. My grandmother learned
to live with the fact that her husband
was really in love with Lauren Bacall.
My grandmother raised five children, taught
at the Garfield School, drank whiskey
in the afternoon, and loved her man.

Just a few years before he died
of a disease nobody could figure out,
my grandfather was watching some talk show
and, all of a sudden, there she was.
Lauren Bacall. A little weathered perhaps
but still beautiful in the way that was
hers. In less than ten minutes
he found out her real name was Betty
Perske, her famous "look" was actually
just a case of nerves, and worst of all she was
a Jew. My grandfather never spoke her name
again. When she turned up later
in some interview or even the old films
he simply muttered "Jew" and left
whatever room he was in. I never knew
where he went to, what language
he spoke to himself. All I knew was
that he'd let go of Lauren Bacall
and that he would not take her back.

My grandfather died a day-by-day
kind of death. As though the spirit
waded its way cautiously into deep water.

The words went first. Then the hands.
Then the eyes. At the funeral, the priest
used my grandfather as a metaphor
for the human condition, for the wasting
away, and said religion was the answer.
I could've killed that son of a bitch, death
so close as it was. At least I could've
taken him down to the old theatre in town
and put him in the front row and shown him
Lauren Bacall's first movie. The one
where she says, "If you want me, just whistle;
you know how to whistle, don't you? You just
put your lips together and blow." The priest
might've said, Just put your hands together
and pray. But my grandfather needed something more
as he travelled toward death. Something more certain.

Father, whistle to God and you might make
music. But whistle to Lauren Bacall
and you make love. Whistle in her direction
and you have never made a sound so sure.

Great Uncle Norvell Fast Is Dead

When death won out, Norvell was about 80.
He'd been married a long time to great aunt Kate.
At every family party, after the whiskey
Kate would say that her marriage succeeded
because, each morning, Norvell
would sit on her toilet first, to warm
the seat for her, for great aunt Kate.

Every year, we'd laugh, even though
we thought it was pretty strange. Every year,
Norvell would nod, sip his drink, and say,
"I defy anybody to tell me different:
It's every small gesture of love
that matters. And besides
Kate deserves a warm place to wait
for the everyday coming up of light."

But now Kate, already older than she wants
to be, must also deal with the unbroken chill
of waking. With the long cool night.

On the same day that Norvell Fast died
so, too, did a friend of mine. Out west
where the land is supposed to expand,
my friend stared into his thirtieth year,
into the sun he saw buried in the mountains,
and he decided the next step
was too much, was enough.
So he cut himself away from his legs,
away until blood told him all he thought
he needed to know. He forgot
two children. A woman who loved
him. Forgot about a country
that would've waited for him.

At some point, memory fails many of us.
Maybe it even failed Norvell Fast.
But I doubt it. Even in death's face
I expect Norvell refused to claw
at the earth. More likely, he reached
for a drink, said "I'm still good looking,
I'm still putting my arm around a remarkable
woman who will never stop calling out my name,
I'm riding the edges of the sky, and
I defy, I defy, I defy."

Rising Above the Earth

1

She walks sometimes among the treetops,
moves her suddenly light feet across the high
leaves. She is in mourning for entire continents
being unfastened from the orbit of the earth.
And this is work. So she tries imagining herself
older than the rain in a place where fire
scatters from the sun to ignite each day.

There is an old country hymn she tries to remember,
"When He comes, if He comes, I will greet Him
on a cloud that is floating in the Word." But
who is this Guy? What is this Word? Cary Grant?
Love? Dancing? Fred Astaire? Sex? Sparrow? River?
She puts her head down among the leaves, hoping
they will say something, hoping that here will be
some trembling voice like God. When she hears nothing,
she decides to just hum the song, wordless as this tree
which offers her up so high,
and she remembers she grieves
for whole moments of the earth let loose.

Then she sees herself, a long time before,
in a ferris wheel at the country fair,
when the car reached the pinnacle of its arc,
100 feet high, and how it swayed,
part physics, part sky,
part something that for her went unexplained,
while a man below bought a ticket
and climbed on as she waited, suspended
at the very top of the world.

2

Maybe it was 1970. After work
some of us would pick up a case

of Stroh's that we'd sneak down
to the basement of my parents' house.
Normally, we'd shoot some lousy pool,
lie about who still wasn't a virgin,
and listen to "Don't think twice, it's all right . . ."
turned way down low.
                              But
if my folks were out of town
we'd crank the music up
loud like factory sirens summoning
new shifts or girls' voices whispering yes
to everything we could imagine back then.
We played each electric song I owned,
lip-syncing the vocals, pretending
our pool cues were guitars, for hours
playing music that belonged
to someone else and singing with voices
that were not our own. When it was over
we all looked to sleep and dreams
of women who breathed different
air than we would ever know.
                                      I'll confess
I played lead pool cue, left splinters
in my fingertips, singe marks
on the slick wood—17 years old and ready
to hit the streets. Some guys
my age tried to pretend
their pool cues were long arrows pointed
toward the hearts of pretty girls
or were rifles aimed at ominous trees
in the late light. Either way, they chalked their tips
and let fly. The poor bastards
could not conceive what it was
                              to make music.

3
All music or poetry or properly cut
stone is an ordering
of sorrow. A way to set things right.

4
Not quite a year old, she really liked it
when I'd bounce her on my knee and play
Hank Williams and Ernest Tubb records
and tickle her whenever the records skipped.

I was ten and proud that I was big enough
to raise another human being right off
the ground. When she learned her first words,
"God a'mighty," I taught her how to say

"Goddamn," and she would sing along
to "Kawliga" and "Walkin' the Floor over You"
with all the language she had:
Goddamn. God a'mighty. Mighty damn.

Later, she learned mom and day and sky
and bird and look how fall the rain,
but the first words stay the longest,
work farther into us than all the rest.

When I was ten, I bounced little sister
God a'mighty into air that stood still enough
she almost floated, I swear, as if she knew
the very secret of flight.

5
When she fell, it broke all of her.

Though I held out my arms
as if to catch her, I could
do no more than break
my own fall, hold only
to my own reflection.

When my arms were empty
even of that slight weight
I held
to the shadow sketches
of blonder days.

I held to Monet,
whose work she mimicked,
who painted, she said,
like Hank Williams sang,
sadness blurred in everything.
Monet of the lily pads,
colors anchored
like rain
to the smooth water.

When she fell, I learned
to play four chords
on a real guitar,
my range no longer
unlimited, my voice
my own. And it sings

almost as hers did,
slim wings not much
to fly. Still,
"What a beautiful thought I am thinking,
concerning the great speckled bird.
The great speckled bird sits in splendor,
all surrounded and despised by the mob.
I am glad that I come to your meeting,
I'm proud that my name's of a bird.
When He comes, if He comes, I will greet Him
on a cloud that is floating in the Word. . . ."

The Artistry of Pain

There is always enough hurt
to go around. She knows this.
She thinks it's not enough
to hurt quietly, that to proclaim
is to make less. So

the poet clears her throat, says,
"I would like to read from a series
of poems I have written about
pain." The first involves a man
who has lost the use
of his legs after being hit
by a truck. His boss fires him.
His wife leaves him for the man
who drove the truck. And oh he feels
"the pain, the pain, except
in his toes which he cannot feel
at all."
        Pain, part two, concerns a woman
eaten, but only half way,
by cannibals. She then must watch
as her husband is transformed
into the stuff of bouillabaisse, one
eye staring back at her as if plucked
from a sea bass.
        Her pain is endless
as a drive all the way across
Nebraska. And I leave it there,
dust smoking in the Wahoo fields.

Later, I call my mother, say, "Ma,
I just sat for an hour and listened
to a woman read poems about pain."
Ma says, "You're not
going to marry her, are you?"

My mother likes poems that rhyme,
end happy and neat as old movies.
My mother was pregnant twelve times, felt
four die inside her. She saw two others fade
only a few days into light. She wrote
in her diary that they were small
and the world was big. They lived
long enough to be blessed,
attached to a name, and buried
in solid ground. One more child
lived twenty-five years, remained small
in a big world.
                My mother holds
my father's hand sometimes. Says "Piss"
when she's angry, and bakes an angel food
cake every Christmas for the baby Jesus.
She dyes away the grey in her hair,
sings country songs when she vacuums,
and drinks two Old Milwaukees every afternoon.

Ask her about her life.

She will tell you
her children are handsome, not ridiculously thin,
and smart enough to walk in the right kind
of rain. She is still in love. When she is sad,
it is for others whose lives
have not been so good. The ones
run over on dark streets, who do not have
the strength, audacity, or luck to rise.

Living Will

1

He wants to say,
This is how you save
yourself. He wants to offer
these words to her
like so many
small candles
in the dark back corner
of the church he attends
in memory.
                He wants to say
This is how . . .
                but then
he isn't so certain
what he means. What
ear lobes these words
are meant to nibble on
as the syntax shifts
from verbs
                to nouns.
Away from save
toward shelter, shoulder,
the moon broken in half
above a dirt-roiled field of snow.

2

Unplug me if
the respirator eats and drinks
for me, cries for me
listening to Iris DeMent
or Emmylou Harris sing. Or if,
one day, you never return
from a late afternoon
walk.   Should I be found

comatose
on a trout stream
forty years from now,

leave me there. Pretend
I'm only waiting for you,
that woman I saw once on the stream's
other shore, catching elusive
green boughs, pulling
my shadow as well, siphoning light
from half the moon.

3
And when I give
away that shadow for good,
feed me to ashes
and let the wind hide me
someplace sweet
that you've always wanted
an excuse to visit.
How fine to be reason
for a journey
         and not
the end of the world.

4
But don't let death take me
to Indiana or Ohio or
to any southern fields and towns
that line up east
of Texas.
        I know
Texas is dreary, too, but
I like the food and music
enough to be dead there, no matter
the winter chill of a Baptist rain.

5
Better yet, don't let death take me
at all. That's really what these words

have been after. I want eternity
to kiss my way down the freckles
of your back, to rub your feet
after you and your daughter finish
shoveling snow. I'll cook dinner,
maybe ribs in sesame seeds and
red chilis. In time I want a child of ours
to climb out of your body's hills
to live longer than God.

6
Maybe he could just offer her
fresh peaches. He imagines that nectar
swimming down her chin and
onto her breasts. He could offer
to lick them clean.
There would be that wonderful
flavor of peach and her skin
and even the taste of his own tongue.
Yes, that's all there is to it. He could
offer her peaches. Fresh peaches.

Over the Cookie House

My grandfather Andy Reinhard gave me the first poem I ever remember hearing:

> O little birdie in the sky
> Why did you do that in my eye?
> Now I'm a big boy I don't cry
> But I'm sure glad
> That cows don't fly

I don't think he wrote that, but the stuff of poetry is there, one way or another. (Its influence is certainly apparent in my first poem, about my sixth grade teacher, Richard Bump: "Mr. Bump/has a lump/on his rump.") My grandfather was a cookie salesman, driving the two-lanes of Michigan's upper peninsula and northern Wisconsin, back in the days when you could go to Callahan's Grocery Store and scoop cookies like hard candy out of big bins, back before everything was Nabisco and so much gloss.

When I was four, my family lived for awhile over Andy's cookie warehouse. We wouldn't be there long—the apartment was small and my mother was already pregnant with her third child and there were mice, fat, cookie-fed mice—but I remember Andy taking me on frequent tours of the cookies. Macaroons. Chocolate chips. My favorite, chocolate marshmallow swirls. Windmills, which looked great but you had to pick out the nuts. Strawberry coconut numbers. Fudgies. Cinnamon stars. Butter balls. Pecan sandies. Molasses hermits. My earliest memories spring from those boxes, following a miniature me as I go from one display to the next, sampling all the way along while holding my grandfather's enormous hand.

Andy wasn't literary in the traditional sense, yet I think my love of words, of the places inhabited by words, comes from him. He was a marvelous storyteller, and the sillier the story, the better he told it. While sipping his Canadian blend medicine, he'd let fly, big finishes set up by cigar smoke that I swore he'd inhale and then blow out through his ears. His eyebrows were like chorus girls and there were plenty of leg kicks toward the end of the show. Whenever he talked up his days as star fielder (he never said which field) for the Raggedy Assnines baseball team out of Brimley, he'd haul out this beat-up, grass-stained baseball he kept in a Miracle Whip jar. He held that jar with the same reverence Father Callahan held up the chalice at Sunday Mass (the Callahans were everywhere in those days), and I've come to attach a similar reverence for the jar, disappeared now for so many years.

My grandmother would later tell me Andy found that ball when he was out mowing the lawn. Probably something a kid lost in the high grass.

Most of his stories were recollections of younger days, of pulling down the outhouse while his uncle was there reading the Sunday paper, of dancing Friday nights with my grandmother near Bay Mills and people driving all the way from Detour to watch. I'm sure there was something true in most of those stories; I'm also sure he kept changing them to try to make them true for us as well. Until even I felt like a dancer.

He never talked about being orphaned at twelve, separated from his sisters, then forced to quit school after seventh grade and work in his uncle's hardware store in Brimley. He'd had dreams of being a lawyer, would've been a good one, but he sold cookies instead and learned how to tell stories and sing silly songs about French nurses and beer. One Christmas he gave me presents that included a rusty can of turtle soup and some Red Owl peas (a vegetable that made me throw up). Later Christmases, my brother Matt usually gave him some hemorrhoid cream, and in 1979 I gave him a wide tie, the lining of which was a photo of a very naked woman. He thought this an exceptional gift, and my grandmother had me wear it to Andy's funeral in 1984; shortly afterward my ultrareligious Aunt Ann unknowingly donated the tie to the St. Vincent de Paul Society. I haven't worn one since.

Even when the anti-Semitism of his last few years put a sad edge on too many of his words, I couldn't help but love the way his eyes continued to light up when he told stories (by this time he'd switched from Canadian whiskey to gin). I never saw him treat anyone less than decently, and he remained a beautiful dancer. As much as I hated the poison that became a part of him, I couldn't help but love him.

Most of us who fiddle around with words are asked, "Why do you write?" The person who asks this question usually does so in a tone you'd think would be reserved for people who spend their free time skinny-dipping with tiger sharks. So not too long ago somebody asked, again, "Why do you write?" and I offered the following response:

I write for love? Of course. A love of women, river and prairie and mountain, family, words, the spin of the earth around me. Writing is a celebration of what I love, an exploration—however clumsy—of that love. It's a way to love more fully, even when love has failed me or I've failed love. I also write for money—about $12.09 for every week of my adult life so far. Almost beer money if I were to drink Old Milwaukee.

Writing offers me a voice I don't find anywhere else. And there are countless canyons that somehow give that voice a resonance, a response. I'm by nature shy, an awkward dancer (unlike my grandfather, graceful in his suspenders and black shoes). Writing's my confidence, my metronome for the long waltz.

Poetry offers me a chance to latch on, for an occasional moment, to some of the world's rhythms—that notion courtesy of Wordsworth, Williams (Hank), and Norman Maclean. Poetry like trout fishing and making love and tickling a baby and learning how to laugh in sad times. Poetry is often an attempt at ordering sorrow, to give form to loss. But I also write for the power of resurrection—the power, even in a piece such as this, to retrieve some of the people and things and emotions lost to this evaporation of days in which we live.

Looking over this response to that old question Why, I realize I'm doing what my grandfather did, trying to find reasons for celebration, trying to tell stories from some true point in my life, telling those stories in such a way that the truth might become someone else's. And like Andy, I often start my stories by focusing on family and seeing where their voices will take me, including some voices that can only speak if I listen.

I frequently tell that poem of my grandfather's to college students, especially those who either fear poetry or grew up around cows. Better yet, my nieces Beth and Becca memorized it last Christmas. Oddly enough, though, I've never had much of a yearning for cookies since those early days over the cookie warehouse. Maybe I ate too many swirls. Maybe imagination's collaboration with memory prevents any other cookies from being as rich or tasty. Maybe it's the absence of my grandfather's hand holding mine and leading me along.

FOR JAKE'S SAKE

Scott W. Wrobel

> "Get up on your feet,
> up on your feet,
> 'cuz it's a new day coming."
> —*Theme song from "One Day at a Time"*

Jake throws his library books on the counter and pulls a note off the refrigerator. "There's a chicken dinner in the freezer," it says, and "Sometimes I think this world is another planet's hell."

He puts his mom's message in his back pocket, grabs a Post-It note from the junk drawer, writes, "I know every theme song to every show on TV," and puts it on the refrigerator.

He throws dinner in the microwave.

His mom doesn't cook because she's a psychologist. His dad doesn't cook either. He's a senator. He eats out, has cocktails and networks.

Once he networked on Mom's face.

One of Mom's notes said, "None of us live up to God's high ideals. Dad is not a bad man. He's just a man with frailties." Jake wrote back, "We're movin' on up, to the East Side, to a dee-lux apartment in the sky."

After three minutes, Jake pulls his dinner from the oven.

He sits at the foot of the table. He likes the inside of the chicken and the crunchy ice-chunks of corn.

Dad's not home but he lives there. Behind Jake's chair is proof, a path in the carpet where Dad paces with the phone. It runs from the family room down the hallway to the bathroom where he talks while peeing. Jake's supposed to admire that he can talk and pee at the same time because it's an example of Dad being his own person.

I'm my own person and I don't give a shit what anybody else

thinks," Dad sometimes says while preening his perfect mustache in the mirror. It's his favorite line.

Jake writes another note while eating, "In the theme song of "Leave it to Beaver," they just whistle. The same goes for "My Three Sons" except they also snap their fingers and that's what makes the show its own show."

Across from Jake is Dad's chair, the head of the table.

Dad once said, "A foot can't work without a head."

"Or without another foot," Jake said.

"Don't get smart," Dad said.

Behind the "head" on the wall are pictures of Jake's smiling sisters. When Dad's at the table, they laugh at him behind his back.

The good sister is at college making the family name look good while the bad one is busy dragging it into the toilet, "the head." She has purpose. Jake's not supposed to admire her.

Jake thinks his bad sister, Janice, looks like Barbara from "One Day at a Time" except she's taller. She lives with a guy name Reg who has a van and a pool table.

She came home two weeks ago when the senator was in D.C. She kept her eyes on the front door and listened for door-slams in the garage even though Dad was on C-Span, live.

Jake's mom said, "Dad's not a bad man. He's just got the frailties of a human being and that can't be helped."

Janice took Jake for a walk and said, "Mom's crazy, Jake."

Jake said, "But is she her own person?"

"No," she said. "I don't think so."

***

The week after that Jake's good sister, Jenny, came home from school and took him out to eat. Jake thought she looked like Natalie from "Facts of Life." She ate salad. Jake ate a cheeseburger.

"Mom isn't crazy," she said. "She's just got the frailties of a human being and that can't be helped."

Jenny is learning to be a psychologist like their mother.

"They still fight all the time," Jake said.

"It's not your fault that they fight," Jenny said.

"Who said it was?"

"No one," she said.

"Then why'd you say it like it could be true?"

Jenny went back to college.

Jenny says she's grown in awareness since she distanced herself from the dysfunctional nuclear unit. Janice says she wants to kill the senator and commit Mother. Jake says he's not allowed to watch the "Carol Burnett Show." He has a private picture of his sisters from when they were alone at the Minnesota State Fair. He's hardly seen at all because they were smothering him with hugs.

A stranger took the picture and said, "Precious."

Jake said, "I'm so glad we had this time together."

Janice's chair is to Jake's left, Jenny's to his right. Mom has no chair. She's busy healing lives, and when she's home she's busy getting all those things done that would never get done if she didn't do them.

Her favorite line is, "I am not a slave," which she often shouts while vacuuming.

Once she caught Jake reading "Playboy" in the garage. Jake said, "This isn't a 'Playboy,'" and she said she believed him because she had to protect her sanity.

Jake thinks to himself as he eats his chicken, "I'm not eating chicken," then thinks, "I'm not thinking because I'm in another planet's hell."

He finishes dinner and goes to his room, shuts the door. Mom and Dad get home around seven to "make love," a term he knew from a book Jenny once let him read.

She said, "It's natural to explore your sexuality. There's nothing to be ashamed of."

"Who said there was?" he said.

"No one," she said.

"Then why'd you say it like it might be true?"

The book said, "Some partners enjoy painful acts of intercourse while others receive pleasure by fantasizing about pain during acts of penetration or by 'talking dirty.'"

It always sounded like things crashing to Jake.

He lies on his bed and writes a letter to his bad sister in red pen. "We got different strokes to move the world," he writes, "even if this world is another planet's hell! Just the good old boys, never doin' no harm."

Mom put a clipping under his door last night that read, "Freedom hath a thousand charms to show/That slaves contented never know."

Jake wrote back, "I can name the real names of every character on every show currently on TV."

The front door slams. Jake feels it in the mattress springs. He enters the closet, digs in. He's got a blanket and a small TV he cradles between his knees. He turns up the volume to kill the living room lovemaking but keeps it down enough so he won't miss something important.

"I've had it. I'm done. I'm done."

"I'm getting tired of hearing this."

"I mean it, goddamn it."

"Then do it instead of talking."

"You'd like that."

"Don't do me any favors."

"The only reason I'm staying is for Jake's sake."

When he hears the liquor cabinet hinges squeak, Jake turns up the TV—Johnny Fever is passed out on Mr. Carlson's couch—but the bad volume also rises. He doesn't have controls for that. He turns off the TV. The TV won't work anymore.

Looking into the dark, Jake thinks about a sensory deprivation chamber he once read about in the encyclopedia. He thinks he should build one. His closet has darkness but is sweaty, musty, and lets in too much noise.

Thumps on the floor and the hallway walls, voices muffled and sharp from the bedroom. Jake grits his teeth. Mom once wrote, "The wicked often work harder to go to hell than the righteous do to enter heaven." Jake was months from seventh grade, but he understood the messages, most of them.

He made his own. "It's you girl, and you should know it...We're gonna make it after all." But Mom never commented. She did her own thing.

Jake crawls from the closet. He doesn't know why. He never crawls out until they make the moaning bedroom love and go dead. Usually, he stays in the closet all night.

Opening his desk drawer, he scoops a pile of Post-It notes from his mother into a shoe box and reads them to drown out the noise.

He reads, "Those who deny freedom to others deserve it not for themselves." Jake knew Abe Lincoln from the mountain where Dad took his picture. It was a fun vacation. Jake didn't know any better.

A voice from the other room says, "Then do it, goddamn it!"

Jake reads, "A good marriage would be between a blind wife and a deaf husband." He smiles.

He's sick of his room.

He walks down the hallway without tiptoeing, past the noisy lovers. He picks up the phone and dials his bad sister.

"Is Janice there?"

"She's sleeping," says the guy with the van. "Everything cool, Jake?"

He dials his good sister.

He hears more crashing down the hall in the bedroom. The senator's making a speech.

The voice in the phone crackles, "Jake?"

"Jenny," he says. "I just read something. 'No man thoroughly understands a truth until he contends against it.'"

"What are you talking about?"

"'Who is more foolish, the child afraid of the dark or the man afraid of the light?'"

"Where's Mom? Put Mom on, Jake."

"'Faults are thick where love is thin.'"

"Are they fighting, Jake?"

"'A tendency to self-destruction seems to be inherent in the overdeveloped human brain.'"

"Who said that, Jake? Speak."

"'If one has truly lost hope, one would not be on hand to say so.'"

"Shhh, Jake, listen."

"Mom wrote this one to me twice," he said. "'In the fight for survival, a tie or a split decision simply will not do.' What does that mean?"

The far end of the house shakes. Jake drops the phone.

He picks up the phone.

"Jake, what's going on?" She's crying.

"Listen to this one Mom gave me this morning..."

"Call 911, Jake. Call 911, please."

"'If you can't get rid of the family skeleton, you may as well make it dance.'"

Deborah Cummins

Nothing's Safe

Not the hammer, claw variety,
I used yesterday to hang a photograph,
not the garden trowel,
its innocent flat face
offering one final tamp
to Purissima and Dreaming Maid.
Not safe those coiled hoses
collecting dust in the rafters
of my father's garage, once a paradigm
of precision, that procession
of shelved Gerber jars, nuts and bolts
sorted each according to size and function
like bleached spectators witnessing
the wizardry of his hands.

My father's hands,
gilded one Saturday like the motes
encased by a band of sunlight
which through one spotless window
found the bench and cut it
with a razor's accuracy into halves.
How was it possible?
Those same hands
five days a week thrust elbow deep
into vats of bones and blood,
skinning, kneading, stuffing
wads of meat into gut.
Hands that could've done anything:
played Bach or Mozart,
probed a damaged brain,
focussed a microscope lens
on a Petri dish of fungi,

pitched the bottom-of-the-ninth,
bases loaded, three-two count fastball
to the league leading batter striking out.

Hands that lifted me onto a fence post,
opened in my direction
as he stepped back, said, "Jump."
How quickly they disappeared
into pockets, how quickly
he walked away, how hard
the ground came up to meet me.
How he said he'd taught me
a lesson in trust.

One Million Rwandan Refugees Flee To Zaire
Three Hundred Haitians Capsize at Sea
Sarajevo Sniper Kills Fourteen

You and I could've lived
at opposite poles of the planet.
To never have met as likely.
I need to remember Vermont,
that summer we sat on a hill
above a lake so brilliant
it looked oiled
and the sun gilded every hair
on your arm and cheek.
Peach juice dripped from your chin.
We planted the pit,
presumed it would never grow,
but who knows? It takes faith.
The kind which makes it easy
to close my eyes each night, say,
"See you in the morning."

Robert Edwards

The Mud Lake, Minnesota, Poetry Reading and Church Social

Notebooks and potato salad, manuscripts and meatloaf, sonnets and balled up tissues pulled out of apron pockets. A token howl of feedback from the microphone—something to cue the wolves—and the Reading begins...

One of the Mad Poets is reading from *The Beatitude of Babies*. The curtained words wobble apart to reveal a rosemalled heaven of cribs in golden rockabye Sunday afternoons and first words. It's a given there's no baby shit at 4 a.m., or the temper tears of toddlers stamping their feet No! No! No! Fifteen poems to Jesus, five times as many as nails, because the red and wicked world is jumping and twitching in the heat of its own death and happy to be burning and needs to be poemed and prodded to the hickory switch of our Savior. And now come couplets in true red, white and blue. Town ladies and farm ladies get this tingling in their Deuteronomy when the flag goes up the pole!

The Catholics have their bingo and their statue of Mary in a washing machine surrounded by flowers. (Our Lady of the Kelvinator, O Virgin of the Westinghouse, Mother of Whirlpools—wash, rinse and spin our sins away!) The Baptists have their choir and their whiskey in the barn, and the Methodists have preachers with degrees and pews waxed to a slippery gloss. These gray haired grand dames have all done the tour of the Great Museums of Minneapolis and know there is nothing better than potluck and rhymes in the basement of Our Lord O' the Lakes Lutheran Church. Pastor Jim Gunderson knows he'd better lend a hand with the paper plates or else the ladies will be mighty miffed.

If only we could hear odes to casseroles and fresh laundry on the line, go walking beans with the scansion of a hoe or hear a prosody of peas with butter yellow as dandelions in July, a counting of beets per measure. Fast forward to canning time, go down to cellars and count jars dark with pickles, tomatoes red as showroom tractors, edible bullion of corn. Farm accidents and shirts they sew for one armed sons, daughters who keep trying to come home, husbands growing strange by trouble light or dear with decades of casual kindness.

No, these women of Mud Lake will stay Indies in our time, but they have gifts of labor and endurance I wish that they would celebrate and share. I know these women, who know working in the rain, who get up before even dreams of warm milk and watch deer cross green fields of oats. I wish they would come with loaves of poems as high as their white bread comes from the oven.

One by one they leave loud houses, go down to the riverside and are laid under flowers, in American earth, their great singing clans above them, treasuring their recipes, their eyes and smiles alive in wild little girls reading poems in trees, chocolate on their chins.

My Uncle, Willis

Growing up, I heard stories of men
going barn to barn to talk by lamplight
in the North Dakota of the 1920's.
Or men just walking down dirt roads,
either toward or away from their families,
limping into a dusty yard full of chickens
to ask for water and a little fried cornmeal mush.
Kids behind her skirts,
my grandmother negotiated chores for meals,
knew when to take the safety off the shotgun
and when to relax around knives.
America rode running boards to jazz and rum
somewhere east or west of bankruptcy.
Depression came early to the Plains.

Grunting sows and blizzards, my grandfather
mailing home his logging camp pay, and everywhere
women and children holding down the farms.
A young woman when she'd come to the prairie,
with more tears already dried behind her
than my grandfather would ever know
she watched foreclosure auctions turn ugly,
waved goodbye to families rattling down
dirt roads past fields that failed
and the dead they left behind.

Four children of her own, a nephew and a niece,
three-times-a-widow mother-in-law, barbwire
thin kids who wandered farms like cats,
turning wild to kindness. She gave away
her life, out of her hands, one loaf
or stitch in time. Winters picking
the railroad tracks for coal, or summer windmills
grinding dry horizons, and my grandfather

returning, leaving on a wind
dark with earth, laundry coming down clean
only in the clothes-pin marks. Pregnant
again, my grandmother hauled water,
slopped hogs, gave up dusting.
The youngest then, my uncle, Willis,
made the bearable beautiful—sweet little boy
running into her arms, climbing
into her aproned lap with words of love,
and she rocked him, sang him to sleep
while the earth rose over the house...

He died of whooping cough the day
my uncle, Chuck, was born. Sedated
and rambling, in the first delivery room
she'd known, she begged God to take
the new baby, take chickens, hogs, farm
and husband, but leave her Willis. God
opened gates of pain, left her
with that wounded truth to bury one
and nurse another. The prairie light
came down to the last hog loaded on a truck
and nothing else to sell, no labor equal
to the dust black as Bibles.
She waved goodbye to a woman standing
on a dirt road, worried apron full of wind.
After that, my grandmother hated the Plains,
a hardscrabble place that kept her angel's grave—
a photograph she wept over: a small headstone
of a lamb, taken from a perspective of the knees.

But the children who were born there remember
picking wildflowers growing between the stones
of Indian fires still blackened under cottonwoods
in the coulees. Children know who is loved the best,
and invent a place at the edge of earshot to outgrow
legends who never lived to make the usual mistakes
or travel the distance to a mother's silence.

In her last years, when I was a boy,
my grandmother studied Heaven like a job

by lamplight in a time of television wars
and riots and rockets rising on fire
toward the moon—a time she never understood
except by way of Revelations. My uncle, Chuck,
excelled at everything, moved away and became
the family's cryptic model of money,
style and success. Behind electric gates
in California, he knew his birthdays made her cry,
setting one age against another,
and how she dreamed past all her pride in him
to Willis, who might have been illiterate
and swept a floor and still kept all her love.

When she spoke of death, looking forward
to mercies and rewards for a faith held hard
as whispered hymns against the years of snow,
it wasn't my grandfather she'd see
and be a wife again, not father or mother,
sisters or brothers, lost friends standing
on a dirt road, waving hello, not even
Jesus opening the light. It was her Willis
whom she'd sing to sleep again, rocking him
in her young mother's lap, the prairie,
the harvest prairie, and the sky blue
as wildflowers, held in the forever of a Heaven
like North Dakota in the 1920's.

Tom Hansen

Those Long Days Things Go Wrong
For Bruce Polay

A gust of wind—
sheets of paper panic;
drops of midnight rain
squeeze in through the screen.

I sigh and get down on all fours:
good dog Tom, the paper herder.

Back on my desk,
they flap and hyperventilate.
I try to calm them down.
To hold my breath. To write....

So why go on like this?
Why leave the window open?

Because I hear a piano playing
out there in the dark and rain.
The wind that blows my papers off
blows some Chopin in.

Because it just
comes down to this:

between the thing we try to do
because "I do this; this is me"
and the nothing we get done
those long days things go wrong,

there sometimes comes a little stream
of midnight Chopin bright with rain.

L.L. Harper

Hollis

our dog seems hypnotized by lace
curtains that seem to float
away from the dining room window.
They drift light as steam,
whiter than that and undulate
like a half-dressed woman
with a secret.

Hey Hollis! Wake up!
Look. Spring springs,
when everything merely adequate,
even you and me maybe,
might be mistaken for the amoral,
the arresting, the affluent.
Why not?
Forget winter.
Forget cleaning up,
forget scrubbing down.
Run with me, now,
through the house, the yard,
the neighbor's yard too,
the neighbor who hates our dog.
It is Kerouac's spring and we need
to decompress our lungs,
feel them rise like the curtains
at the window, like kites
hell-bent for the wake
Icarus traced in his heroic meltdown.
I don't know about you Hollis,
but I need to fly with any bird
that will have me,
surging and falling
like a swelled sail,
dirigible me
and my dirigible heart.

Their Fathers Were Beautiful

No children,
Ruby claims,
worth keeping.
But she's delivered four
I know of which always amazed
me in the wake of her stunning homeliness.
Their fathers were beautiful,
she admits and I believe her because
each child could be Raphael's.
Her own charms still glow
like a votive candle
under smoked glass.
After two cups,
the red wine trips
a hidden mechanism that
turns her back twenty years
and the flush to her cheeks
becomes irresistible as peaches,
lush and ready to be picked.
When I tell her this,
she takes my hand to her breast,
soft as excelsior,
and tells me if I was a man
oh, she would show me
a thing or two,
and I can't help but believe her.
In the glow of her quiet burn,
I'm convinced.

Jeanne Lyon

Looking for a Heart

A looking goes on like a furtive touching
when we walk at the grocery, noticing
we're buying the same Kellogg's Corn Flakes
and frozen Pizzas for One. The look
spans aisles and slips around corners
to the next, where there might be a smile
or a stolen glance at more
than just the manly-smelling
Dove he's selected.
                Then it's off
to the filling station, where I serve myself
but over the acrid smell of gasoline
the lanky blue-uniformed man chats
and cleans my windows, commenting
on the weather, telling me to have a good one
as I leave and feel him squeeze
the seat of my blue jeans with his eyes. Men.
                At the bookstore
the man of my dreams browses beside me
in Poetry—tweedy, fair-haired,
high-browed, long-legged, politely
rumpled. We exchange a nod. Then
a gold ring flashes at me and leaves, taking
the next-to-last copy of Keats with it.
I didn't come here for Keats, but now
I think I'll read Keats, nothing but
Keats, for a long time.
                I begin
with my new-bought book
over coffee next door, and this time
a guy in a t-shirt climbs down a ladder
from changing a light bulb,
like one of the angels Jacob saw

descending from heaven, and says he'd like to read
some of my poetry. That sends me running home
to write some for him. Men.
                          I love them,
their endless variety, and I think
of them as I carry out the last box
of my ex-lover's magazines, struggling,
when along comes a man in a backward Broncos cap
and takes it for me, smiling.
I think perhaps they're indestructible.
Or maybe not:
                     I can remember
in the darkness after sex
the regular thumping of a heart
beneath my ear
and the soft way a voice
rumbled into life, from somewhere
close to the thumping

Jim Murphy

October Sunbath on the Practice Field

The air waves
are humming with this
bright message,
and an unseen
marching band is
at practice, ol' varsity
coming across the years
to where our sweaters are coiled
nonchalantly in the dead grass.
More sun-shards appear in
glaring chrome, metal
pens, the starkness of paper
where illicit black lines
are none too discreet
in the scrawling, etched
definition of this autumn light.
It's too late in the year to believe
the good, half-burnt salt
of my own baked skin.
After some vapid remark
about the climate change,
I ask if you hear the bass drum's
muted marching pulse,
calendrical, coming over the trees.
The instant of your moving
to hear, your slow lean into the
welcome broadness of the noon air
rings with an ephemeral grace
that makes me swallow
all my dross and slippage,
proposing, convincing
that this is summer thirst.
And the good times
run back to us,
and through us,
and up into the wind.

Howard Nelson

The Buck

We almost didn't see him
as we walked along the path, talking—
not thirty yards away, on a little rise,

tall among the brush, the buck,
with his crown of curved prongs. Not hard to understand
why men once wore those arcs above their heads.

He stood in the green dusk—
that sculpted rack, his brown
so light and warm,

head held high
and angled from his body.
He didn't move at all, not even an ear.

He looked at us with his whole body.
After a minute of this, I thought,
we are giving him a bad lesson about human beings,

so I stood on a big rotting log and said,
"If I had a bow or a rifle, and if I wanted to kill you,
you would be gone, all your sleekness

would be on the ground, no more
beautiful does for you!"
And still he stared, even when

I raised my arms, and only when
I stepped off the log
and started walking toward him

did he wheel and crash away through the brush.
Next winter he will probably be killed.
To kill him will be no small thing.

To take those antlers from him will be no small thing.
It will be like drinking blood,
but no one will think too much about it,

except maybe in some back corner
of the skull where laughter
and the rush of pleasure darken.

Eating Eggs

It bothered me, when I was a kid,
the way my father ate eggs.
The way eating absorbed him—
the way he would push the home fries into the spilled yolk
with little clicking motions of his fork—
how serious he was about it—
the way he slurped his coffee
and mopped up the yolk so thoroughly with the toast
and stuffed it in his mouth—
and the way he drained his cup
and set it definitely down on the saucer
as if he had really accomplished something.
Ah, the satisfaction and smallness of his pleasure!

And now
whenever I go into some small restaurant
and order eggs, home fries, toast, and coffee,
as this morning, with rain teeming down on the pavement
beyond the plate glass
of The Rosebud,
as I push the potatoes across the plate
into the bright yellow pool,
I think of him, and love him
and his clicking happiness.
Whenever I eat fried eggs alone,
with pleasure,
I am with him.

Linda Goodman Robiner

High School Sex

Boys looked at her in her sweaters.
She wanted them to look.
Circular stitching on Vassarette bras
embellished her pointy nipples.

A couple of boys tried to finger
the softness of the surface.
Though she wanted to be fondled,
she pushed their hands away.

Seventeen warned *Once you start
you'll never be able to stop.*
She saw herself rolling downhill,
a mythic figure, never stopping.

All the girls were virgins then.
That's what they told her.

Pretzels in Bed

My husband hung his pants in the closet
    as soon as he took them off,
crammed shoe trees into every polished shoe,
couldn't stand when I went barefoot,
always washed his hands before dinner,
hated when I ate pretzels in bed,
refused to go to a party with me
if I wore the dress with just one sleeve.

I celebrated the divorce with a party,
draped golden glitz over my curtains,
served paté in the shape of a hedgehog
    and goblets of champagne,
sprinkled fairy dust in my hair that
fell onto my lashes,
set out a crystal bowl of sparkles
    with a silver brush for my friends.

Fairy dust lingered on the floor for weeks.
I tracked it into my bed.

Matthew Spireng

Cabbage Whites

Whether it was the white wings, erratic flight,
or simply that so many seemed to be,
as a child I chased cabbage whites
across the weedy lawn one late May day
and captured in my hands as many beating wings
as came in reach and, counting all I caught,
squeezed them in a jar, the lid kept close
so none could fly away. How I counted
mating pairs, I can't recall, though then
I thought them Siamese twins. The captured
filled the jar and fluttered there till
it seemed as light as light itself,
though when I loosed the lid to let them out
a few had died. The air, my hands, the jar
stayed heavy with the scent
of wings of cabbage whites.

MUTATIONS

Marianne Barnett

My brother Phil sat up in his sleep every night at the stroke of midnight and screamed at the top of his lungs.

"It's all those war games," Mother would say, at the breakfast table. One year after another. One morning after another. Mother saying, "Things catch up to you."

Phil would say, "I cannot remember."

Mother saying, "Every night. It's the same. War and terror. Quit playing all those games."

Phil would say, "I cannot remember."

We quietly ate our breakfast.

All of us in the middle of childhood. Phil swearing that he slept through the night. Every midnight the same. He cannot remember.

Now with my feet suspended above the level of my heart. Finding myself somewhere in adulthood. After surgery. My feet wrapped in gauze. The blood pooling below. I hear Phil in the night air. Bellowing. He is sitting up in his sleep.

At midnight, I sit up. At first, for a few nights after the surgery, I take a pain pill.

"Pain has never been proven to actually exist," my podiatrist said. We were halfway through the surgery. Halfway through fifteen shots into my ankles. Halfway to the distilling numbness.

"Are you telling me that there is no such thing as pain?" I asked. I stared then at the three white figures standing over my ankles. One podiatrist, two nurses. Huddled in a mass.

"Nothing but childbirth could be worse," Bonnie, my therapist, said. "Maybe," I said.

"That is the problem with surgery. It appears to be a quiet dream," Bonnie said.

"Maybe," I said.

Bonnie sees me week after week in her small upstairs office.

Every Tuesday I sit with my back to the window and look at her. Every Tuesday I sit thinking of Fred, our marriage, and the day he said, "Do you realize you haven't talked to anyone in three weeks?"

I said, "Tomorrow is Monday. Take out the garbage."

"Find someone to talk to, Maggie. Whatever the hell it is," Fred said.

"What can we work on today?" Bonnie will say. She says this every week. After the week's events are discussed. Idle gossip about the community as if we are at a cocktail party. Then when the air settles, she will say, "What can we work on today?" The weeks can come and go like this. Weeks later, it would be my foot surgery. Bonnie knows feet. Last summer she stepped on a quilting needle buried in the carpet. All the way through her big toe. And the blood. All the blood.

"I fainted, you know, right there on the table when he put that long needle into my skin," Bonnie said. "And that's when I told my doctor that I would rather have a baby than have another one of those shots in my foot."

It was a good time then. Bonnie and I had that to talk over. One hour in three years we had that much to do.

All the years before this one, Bonnie asking, every week, "What can we work on today?"

Most Tuesdays, I say, "I just want to sit." And that was so after Fred left. After the marriage. After I looked in the yellow pages and flipped a coin to decide on a therapist. Each coin falling sharply in Bonnie's favor. A name printed on a page.

So we sat for an hour every week for over three years. Until the last Tuesday. The last Tuesday before I climb out of bed and head down the road. On that day I said, "Bonnie, I need to let go." Bonnie nodded her head. And then later that evening, when the children had been put to bed and I stared at the television, Bonnie called to say, "I will miss our hour."

All the stories too. The hours sifting through the silence while Bonnie was patient for me.

At first I thought it was surgery that brought me to this pillow. The feet and all. Timing is eveything, one could say. And this can be, really, no exception. I seem to hear what I had long ago given up. I could say that it sounds this way or that. I could even imitate the long echoing bellow. But finally, here in this room, with gauze surrounding the tissue, I am content with what appears to be silent. Even at midnight.

So it began, after the foot surgery, to be told. On a Tuesday in Bonnie's office. I said, "Phil, over childhood, collected plastic army soldiers and other miscellaneous game pieces which he drafted into war."

"War?" Bonnie asked.

"Could we have called it anything else?" I asked.

I told Bonnie how Phil would stage battles in the dirt pile next to the garden behind our family home. On one side of the cherry tree, Phil lined up green plastic soldiers knee high in the dirt. On the other side, blue plastic soldiers. If it wasn't the cherry tree, it was Phil's bedroom with the Risk game, or any other game pieces strategically settled into piles around his bed. It was tedious warfare. All the games gathered into one location. And it was a solitary affair.

"Solitary?" Bonnie asked.

"We weren't invited," I said.

"Still, it might matter," Bonnie said.

And because it was almost through, our Tuesday hour, I told her about late summer afternoons. Sundays. The day spent in whiffleball. Father taking a nap. His window open to catch the breeze and our voices carrying quarrels of foul plays or runaway balls that travel over our roof and into the street. Occasionally my father standing near the window. He is wiping his face with a wet wash cloth. He is saying through the screen window that if we yell one more time he will take the ball inside.

After naps, after games, on Sunday afternoons, our family sitting attentive and straight against my mother's stiff dining room chairs. One family member passing rice and gravy to the next. My father with his head bowed. Over his plate. It is long after the blessing. He studies his food. Sometimes he points. His finger stretched over his plate. He gets the salt or the pepper shaker or whatever else happens to be in that direction.

Bonnie looked at me as if she were there in the long afternoon. It was easy then to tell her how things accumulate speed, how one story can be told out of nowhere. An ordinary Sunday. My brother Patrick saying, "If there was a war and nobody was left except the dog and Phil, and they held an election, the dog would win."

My father looking up from his plate. And other family members with faces full of food. We are laughing. My father smiling.

Now it is the same after every Thanksgiving dinner blessing. When we gather again in the old house. Perhaps my sister will say, "Remember that story Patrick told about Phil. Tell that one Patrick. The one about the dog and war."

"Phil refused to weed around the trees," Patrick will say.

Phil will say, "It's been fifteen years."

"Mother never once put a stop to this. He could slide out of all his family chores," Patrick will say.

"It's been fifteen years," Phil will say.

"Unbelievable," Bonnie said.

"That is why I never told you this. How could anyone understand?"

"Did Phil ever mow the lawn?" Bonnie asked.

"That is exactly why Mother finally came down hard," I said.

Mother wanted Phil to give up the war games in the dirt patch, to take up friends and God. In a final summer effort, our last days of childhood, Mother poured gasoline over his tricycle axles to remove the oil. Then the wheels squeaked wherever Phil went. So Phil rode to the end of the driveway and then headed down hill until the squeaking wheels scattered into the air. All through childhood, Phil riding squeaking wheels. Once to the neighborhood church where inside he repeatedly stabbed the picture of John the Baptist baptizing Jesus.

"That in itself might be a powerful statement," Bonnie said.

Then our hour was over. Three years to come this far. Tuesday after Tuesday sitting quietly with nothing but cocktail gossip. Who would have known that we had this foot thing in common. Needles in the ankle. Blood at our feet.

And then I am home again. After the Tuesday hour. Where I lie in my bed, feet high, a low throb, and hear all that dinner talk. The first night or so, all that talk sounds more or less like a slow faucet drip. Like the drip you keep running when your pipes threaten to freeze shut in the dead of winter. All that dinner talk. First, the war games, the stabbing, and the years since. That was before the Fred years. Now that dinner talk includes the Fred years.

That is what I told Bonnie the next Tuesday. One story taking on another. One Tuesday melting into the next. Fred, who left one day with his clothes in a box and his albums in paper grocery sacks.

Stacked in the back of his light blue Chevy pick-up. At first it seems a simple thing, I told Bonnie. After the potatoes are served. After Phil announces he wants to marry.

"Tell him, Maggie. Tell him about Fred. That marriage of yours. Tell Phil how difficult it is to live with someone who isn't right, who doesn't think on our level, who will later deprive him of a satisfying conversation after dinner," Mother will say.

I will say, "Marriage isn't what it's cracked up to be."

And Phil will say that he wants to marry despite this. Our voices linger beyond this into dessert where we might discuss the gas station where Phil works for Patrick.

Bonnie said. "Did you confront the situation?"

"I couldn't anticipate dessert coming so quickly," I said.

I knew then that after the foot surgery, after the midnight scream story, it was only a matter of time before Bonnie and I looked right at the marriage.

Bonnie said, "What can we work on today?"

It seemed the likely thing to tell after she had told me her needle through the toe story. We had shared that kind of intimacy then. So I told her that one July, Phil married. He walked down the grass path roped off with blue ribbons. That July was humid. And that night the sunset glowed like hot embers. His bride smiled triumphantly over the small group of friends who perspired on their foreheads and under their armpits where the moisture made half moons on their cotton shirts. The bride's family hugged her after the ceremony. My family stood nearby in case there was something more to be done.

Bonnie asked, "What did you say to this?"

"'She can't read. Not a darn thing in her head,' my sister had said after the ceremony. 'Look what Phil has married.'"

"And really, in the face of this, what could I say?" I said to Bonnie. "I nodded my head." That is exactly what I did. I stood beside my sister after the ceremony and nodded my head.

"Her family is a band of idiots. Not one of them has any ambition, not one respects God, not one," my sister had said. And then the evening was over. The wedding done.

So a summer can go, I told Bonnie. This summer I lie back against my pillow. I rub oil over my stitches, sliced skin, as attentively as a pregnant woman thwarting stretch marks. At first, initially after surgery, I called Bonnie to tell her the day's events, even though it wasn't Tuesday. The need was great. But that had to go. It was enough to hear all the other voices that crowd the day.

My son asks one day late into afternoon, "What did they do?"

I rearrange the blanket. I look up at the ceiling.

"The doctor just cut them off," I said.

"These are uglier feet," he says. He pats my leg the way I pat his when I sit by his bed during a night of fever.

Another day, my daughter. She stares. I watch her curl her hair around one of her fingers. Her fingers are tiny and long. At seven, she believes that life should be one long event in a silk dress with lace and matching fingernail polish. Her first grade teacher, Mrs. Bendall, called last week. She called to tell me that Erin needed to quit fiddling around with her dress during reading. "I am putting her in remedial reading," Mrs. Bendall had said.

I watch Erin looking over my feet. Surveying my taped flesh with the concrete precision of reading *The Little White House*. There have been times when I wanted to tell Erin about Mrs. Bendall. How she will call. I wanted to tell Erin how it feels to be seven. When Mrs. Bendall called, I felt seven. Seven and sitting in Mrs. Hatch's class where I could not write straight r's.

In this bed, I cannot really anticipate anything but the next hour. There is that midnight scream still. It may only be in my mind, but it rings clearly. As clear as the time I sat up in my sleep listening in the dark. After all the years, each night a scream at midnight, no one really looking at the situation, I decided to go into Phil's room and get to the bottom of the matter.

"What is it?" I asked.

Phil grabbed my shoulders and pulled me to his chest. "I have got to get out."

He climbed out of bed and crawled to the wall, slapping the surface. "Where's the door? Where's the door?"

"There's nothing, Phil," I said. I pulled him to his feet and he got back into his bed.

When I told the story, Bonnie broke in with tedious questions. Questions which wear all the edges of a fine story. Doesn't it come down to straight r's, I told Bonnie. All of this movement, all this noise. I told her that story too. And then we came back around to this one. When Phil is back in his bed. After Phil has asked, "What is there?" I didn't answer.

Bonnie interrupting then. I tell her again that I didn't answer. Instead I covered him with the sheet. And Phil slept. In the morning, I remind Bonnie, he will not remember. All those mornings, he does not remember. That is why I couldn't tell Erin that Mrs. Bendall would call.

Now Phil sleeps. So his wife will tell us. It will be over another family dinner. After all the stories. We will hear about the midnight scream, the war games, the dog and final vote story, my marriage to Fred and even the stabbing.

After the stories, over a family dinner, marriages on the table, Phil's wife will say, "He sits up in his sleep at midnight. I touch his back. I tell him to lie down now. So he does."

That is what I want in this room. With my feet on the pillow. After the stories. I want to hear that midnight howl. Bonnie told me that is too much to ask. All this foot talk. Surgery. Our sessions, though, have come down to this. What else is there to get at?

"You can't have bone friction without lubrication finally wearing away," my podiatrist had said. "Cut out a bone and the arthritis will subside. It is in the family genes." That is where the podiatrist began with his thin knife. At the first cut.

I said on that last Tuesday, "Bonnie, what can I say to this?"

And when it came down to each Tuesday lining up into tight-knit rows, I had to call a halt to all this talk, all this noise. And the stories. So it happened one Tuesday. After the usual, "What can we work on today?" Bonnie waiting. The feet at a quiet ebb.

I said, "Time passes."

Bonnie said, "Tell me something I don't know."

I said, "What can I say to all of this?"

And then I told her that the last time I saw Phil was at the gas station. Married now, he looked taller, or something, more mature. That is what I told Bonnie. He put gas in my car and stood awkwardly next to me. And it was cold outside.

I had asked, "Phil, how's married life?"

"Not like I expected." He sounded disappointed, but then in the wind that could easily be mistaken.

And because it was cold and because there wasn't anymore to say I moved away from him and started back to my car.

"No one's there," he had said. I turned and looked at him. And then I got into my car.

"Is that all?" Bonnie asked. "After all these years?"

"I can't come any closer to this story," I said. And then I knew what we had left to say. Tuesdays. All of those afternoons sitting and listening. I would finally have to say, "Bonnie, I have to let go." And now for this foot thing to be so prominent. It left me nothing else to consider.

One night after the bandages are replaced twice and I can walk slowly, I will climb into my car and begin driving down the road. I won't really think I need to end up anywhere, but I'll end up outside the door of an old lover. Someone I haven't seen since my last child was born, since I told Fred to finish the years out on his own. Someone who will know that walking to the front door hurts too much to turn back. So I will stand there in the dark and wait. I will stand there till my feet hurt.

Florence Dacey

Florence Dacey
FEATURED POET

FLORENCE DACEY is the author of two books of poems, *The Swoon* and *The Necklace*, and the recipient of a 1988 Loft-McKnight Award in poetry. Since 1983 she has conducted creative writing residencies in Minnesota schools, as well as workshops and inter-generational projects for teachers, older citizens, and other community groups. She facilitates journal writing workshops for women recovering from abusive relationships and is a consultant in the COMPAS-Blandin Rural Arts Initiative. Dacey lives in Cottonwood, in southwestern Minnesota, and has been active in social justice, environmental, and women's issues for many years.

"Finders/Keepers" and "I Am Cooking" are reprinted from *The Necklace*.

Her House

Our grandma's house was high and dry,
compact as brick,
and there she sat and rocked
amid the ticks of clock.
A house of ears, attic secured
in smells of family pain matured
and settled into rope, wood, oblivion.
She was the house
that fed us pie and slaw.
She was our own mouth
slowed to taste the wedding
of desire and age, not devour.
Around her table we saw our fate
and laughed and ate.
Before her fire we drew the cards.
In her old flesh we hid the words.
And down her steps we must fall.

Finders/Keepers

We know where small things wander
that men and children call for:
keys, pen, shoe. Or cherish:
ring, letter, feather. We know
with our palms and foreheads
because we have touched all these things,
imaged them in particular places—
under the radiator, on the dryer,
behind the tape in the middle right hand
drawer of the cupboard by the back door.

We have needed to remember
when no one else can
where small things come to hide
because we have needed to remember
ourselves, women, disappeared among men and children.

So, when my mother finds
a cherished silver earring I lost
at her house, she calls me
right away on the phone,
oddly triumphant.
I think it is because she has
kept faith in her way
with the small lost truths of women:
that we are each a word
our grandmother, mother dared not say
but could not forget;
that women need one another like water
and what some men call god
nurses the world through our hands and eyes;
that we can find ourselves in any mess

because we are, each of us,
each the separate cherished daughter.
We shine in the mother's skull
till we are found.
We are carried in hands
that refuse to forget
the feel of all
that's small and human-bound.

Swing

The Lake of Childhood
never changes. The Boat,
the Oars, the Rope we pull
rock there and it is still
the Sandbar sweet,
our mother's Voice
across the lap of waves,
our father's Hand
upon the Pier
A Bird wrung from heaven's mercy—

those years of ease set to torn grass
and the child swinging—

But that does change.
For, we remember the child
swinging impossibly
far out over the lake
between the Mother, the Father,
between the stars and heat,
swinging wildly,
stoic.

Our Children

We call in light and wisdom.
We dance around the tree.
Or video or bed.
Be we have to do it.
Because the children are watching,
now more than ever.
Out of the torn corners of their eyes,
they send the birds to spy.
They are the purest terrorists.
Bury it here, quick, bury it even in my chest,
where at least I can make it burn,
make you turn and see, they plead.
Our children with their arrows of grief,
their tender throats in our hands.

On Legs

When she was fifty three
everything ran away like
a pack of crazy dogs.
Her legs began to hurt
more often than not.
She drank, she phoned,
she biked, she schemed.
She danced.
Her legs still hurt but
she danced to Scottish tunes
and American rock and her own
drumming heart.
So sad, so wild it gets
to be when the pack of crazy
people you nursed and dressed
and fed and feted run away.
You can do anything.
You dance on legs that hurt.

I Am Cooking

Watch out! I am burning pans.
I am stirring up trouble
for your empty craw.
I am watching my life simmer
while I tear down herbs
from my drying past.
I chew on three obscene cloves
of garlic. No evil
will befall you.

Oh, my singed meat!
Oh, my bloody bones!

Here in my laboratory
I draw out juices.
My liver and kidneys will
tide you over to Jerusalem.
I stir with my heart, a claw.
My kitchen's a cauldron,
the giant's mouth.
Drop in. Here we
fritter, we stew, we
pickle, fry and render.

Oh, wild scalding in the kitchen!
Oh, thick spoons flying by the windows!

I am cooking here, not my mother.
My breasts are raw. Grease is spitting.
The floor's alive. It croaks and humps.
The table bulges like a mushroom.

My hands are plates. They multiply.
My head is dinner gong.
I strike, I sear
against my family's heat.

Oh, come in to eat, my loves!
Oh, come in to food, everyone!

That Touch

Once we have touched
our dead father's forehead,
we touch everything differently,
especially our past
and the skin of night.

                    Our hands will never be colder.
                    Truth has a new measure.

Trees, he wrote on the yellow-lined sheet.
Inexpensive coffin. His dead body
read like letters he never wrote to me.
One time, we said it, face to face: I love you.
But I was not there to watch my father's mind
collapse like ruined grain. I was making money
planting poems in children's heads.

                    Our hands can only grow older.
                    The truth carry us as treasure.

The oak my father prayed under as a boy dies too this year,
all stripped and sore, surrounded by machines.
The field of ripened wheat he dreamed of called
and, farmer that he was, he went.

He went out, weeping and hollowed.
We sang to him. We raised our limbs
and held the wind and bent to
his coldness, golden, woven,
the simple price he paid, one man's honest wage.

                    Our lives become the tree
                    we lay him in,
                    his hands wrapped round
                    some rooted truth.

When We Ran Out of Land

When we got to the ocean,
there was the dead starfish,
after the sun and temptations of song.
You can't haul a stinking dead starfish
too many miles, so on Ruby Beach
we finally left it, looking like
some impish child peering
from a dead tree trunk.
I have the photos from several angles.
You can tell the starfish knew
the end would be sorrier than we supposed.
All we do is write on sand, grasp for kelp, await the tide.
At one time we could hear each other's encrustation, let us say,
and then somehow we stopped getting just close enough to do that
without ruining anything.
I can't run down this beach anymore
but I still sport with seals
and now you'll see how I, like anemone,
can hold to what my body knows is bed.
I loved the beaches, first of sand,
and father north, of rock.
I even loved when we ran out of land
and had to stop.

Essay

My father, who died in 1992 and felt closer to the gods sitting under an oak tree than anywhere else, believed that your journey through life was preordained. Now that I have lived more than a half century, I can begin to at least see the map. The main route, the side-trips. (I don't believe in dead ends, except as a concept.) My poetry remains the best record of the journey, for me. It's a journey of a woman, American, midwestern, lashed to the times. It's hard not to think in metaphors these days. It seems as if most days are like the extraordinary scene in one of Iris Murdoch's novel where the man gets sucked down into a channel of water with an irresistibly strong current, apparently to disappear into the earth forever, and then ends up thrust through a tunnel to come out with a banged up head and a renewed lust for life. I think I am always deciding whether to sit under this oak tree or jump into the channel, then making some poetry out of the consequences. It's hard work because it's fairly taxing to be alive, aware. Even if it's just your little plot, your little day trip, there's too much going on, too fast or, when you sit, too deeply.

When I was in college, at an unnamed Sexist University, I loved to collect eloquent quotes about art and poetry in particular. I'm not very good at creating my own, though once at a rather dismal in-service I was doing in some school I managed to come up with "I make poetry out of the debris of my life." It's partly true, like many things. There's been a lot of wreckage from a failed marriage. I haven't managed to fashion a remarkable career, either as teacher or writer. Not a very good housekeeper, either. The mess, you know. Moving in the mess, that's what I learned as a woman and mother. The mess of feelings and these blessed children who came out of me and pulled me into new places, over and over, as they sprouted and suffered and called me Mother. Motherhood is the sacrament of failure. They leave us, to pursue their own catastrophes, which may be comforting enough.

I think one of the tasks of the poet is to stay conscious of the contradictions, within and without, and not explode into self-destruction or other more subtle distortions. To enlarge one's consciousness about this is painful. There is enough sadness around to swallow several centuries worth of sensitive people with one gulp. But this is all fraught with humor. That's the salvation of it. (My former Catholicism doth creep in.) If you want to be a poet, it helps to have a myth of some sort and be flexible about changing it. It helps to have a few choice friends who never forget you are a poet and who read your work with loving lively eyes. I would say it helps to have money and time to write, but that would be self-indulgent, wouldn't it?

It's a grave and happy calling, the poet's. You can get away with so much, at least in your imagination. Cry in supermarkets. Miss the point of perfectly clear communications. Say what you take to be the truth in the oddest places and be heard. If you write true poems, strangers will say things to you about your work that will bring tears. This will be something to recall when you are very old. I do think about this now.

I also think I haven't anything profound or new to say about the writing process or the function of poetry or the demise of our civilization. Like most poets I write because I have to, to avoid becoming paralyzed with sorrow and fear, to thwart time and touch someone else, often a woman, as I have been touched. The longer I live, the more layers are available for the poem. There is always the simple risk, though. Risk staying faithful to the impulse, the feeling, the insight that was the conscious start of the poem. Be in love with how you will fail, in as original a manner as possible. Get soaked and wounded and get through and there will be the air and another look. Not to mention the oak tree.

AT JESUS' FEET

Ellen Hawley

The first apartment I ever rented faced a gospel church and a full-sized billboard of Christ, which I looked out at every morning as I drank my coffee. This was no doe-eyed Jesus of the Lambs and Little Children gazing back at me. This was Christ in his agony, twisting against the nails of the cross, his feet pointing limp and white toward accusing Gothic letters that asked, "Is It Nothing To You?"

It was not nothing to me; it was enough that I wedged my chair into the narrow slot between the table and the wall so I'd be less likely to see the billboard when I looked up. It was enough that my eyes turned toward it anyway at least once every meal, then shifted away quickly.

I was nineteen, though, and I'd just moved to the Midwest from New York, so I saw Christ's agony through the romantic sheen which glazed everything that didn't involve my parents. Suddenly no one I knew was Jewish, and that was romantic. And if Christians chose to live next to pictures of men in pain, I didn't criticize them. I was like a tourist, in love with all the local customs. When winter came a full month earlier than I expected it, I was enchanted. The snow fell, then fell again, and fell a third time without ever melting. I watched the driver of a rusty pickup scrape a snowplow blade across the church parking lot, ramming snow into place with the casual grace of a really good auto mechanic, and I believed the driver's thoughts went directly into his muscles and emerged in the form of action. He did none of the weighing and balancing that ate away at my parents' lives. It wouldn't take him three years to decide whether the sofa had one more year of life left in it, and then another year to decide what color the new sofa should be, given that carpets don't last forever but that the armchair was still almost new. If, of course, a new sofa was really necessary.   And once he'd bought the damned thing, he wouldn't shake his head over it and say, "You know, I think that floral print might have been the better buy."

I spent a lot of time that winter sitting sideways on my own couch—a sway-backed survivor of more than one Salvation Army store—looking out the window, past the billboard of Jesus and across the street to the hardware store and the Roundup Bar, where a red neon cowboy tightened a lasso around the neck of a steer in three separate blinks. Sitting there convinced me that I'd changed my life; that I owned nothing worth five minutes' thought, nothing I'd regret leaving behind. In fact I did leave most of it behind less than a year later, which led me to discover that I'd been wrong—I did miss it. Or maybe what I missed was the belief I'd held when I sat in that room: that I could leave my history behind; that the pain of men who drank in bars was nobler than the pain my father felt when he apologized to the landlord that the kitchen sink had sprung a leak; that if I breathed the cold Midwestern air for long enough, it would purify me, freezing out the immigrant's hesitation I was sure I'd inherited from my father. And since the pain I saw in the bar sign, the rusty pickup and Jesus' bare feet wasn't the endlessly apologetic pain I'd grown up with, it seemed diffused and almost kind.

I worked that winter at a small cafe, Andy's, where the only other waitress was a girl who'd just moved to the city from northern Wisconsin. Marlene was a sullen waitress, marking time at Andy's until her older sister could get her on at Dohrn Metals, where the money would be better. She held every nickel tip she'd ever gotten against her current customer, and against the next one, and she took their orders as if they'd interrupted something important. Whenever business was slow, she faded into the kitchen to lean against the wall and smoke, her jaw clenched and her eyes fixed on a point beyond the steaming dishwasher, beyond the kitchen wall, beyond the mud-and-gravel ruts frozen into the parking lot. She smoked without relaxing a muscle, as if even her daydreams gave her something to guard against. And it was this more than anything else that drew me to her: that she was always ready to grab the world in her teeth and shake it.

Marlene was thin, blond and hard-faced, where I was dark and round, too soft yet to understand that talking to the customers wouldn't help either my tips or my disposition. When men told me that what they wanted wasn't on the menu, I blushed and waited until they were ready to order, and they liked me. So while Marlene smoked in the kitchen, I leaned on the counter smiling while some cab driver, or a salesman on his way to one of the factories along Territorial Avenue, asked what nationality I was.

I asked what nationality he thought I was.

Greek, he'd guess, or Italian, or Lebanese. No, I'd say, and no. He'd guess Spanish, Armenian, French, Turkish, Syrian. He'd guess nationalities I'd barely heard of, and I'd say no, and no, smiling, waiting for him to exhaust southern Europe and most of the Middle East so that he had to ask again, what nationality was I?

Jewish, I'd say, and he'd nod and say, Right, he'd thought so. I never asked why he hadn't guessed that. Not because I didn't understand yet about Midwesterners and tips, but because I knew without asking that he hadn't wanted to insult me in case he turned out to be wrong. I recognized this for what it was, but it didn't offend me, because there was never any hostility in the man. And since I'd never been around people who didn't take Jews for granted, I was fascinated.

Marlene knew I was Jewish and we got on well. In the morning we split a sweet roll with butter. If there were any left in the afternoon, we split another. I grew rounder and softer while she stayed angular and kept her jaw clenched against the world.

On the Friday between Christmas and New Year's, we were sprawled out in a back booth toward the end of our lunch break and she tapped a cigarette out as if something in that very pack was going to do her wrong. She blew a smoke ring over my head and I envied her for the perfect way she smoked, for the way she turned away from customers, for being everything I was not.

"In New York," she asked me, "where's your downtown?"

My mind formed a quick picture of the sidewalk outside Klein's at Union Square and just as quickly rejected it. How far downtown *was* downtown? Times Square? City Hall? The Battery? Stretched between New York and the Midwest, the word lost its meaning.

"It's all downtown," I said.

Marlene nodded as if she approved of that and waved the hand holding her cigarette toward the frosted front window, the muddied linoleum and the only customer in the cafe just then, who was hunched over his coffee, his blaze orange hunting cap on the counter beside him.

"What did you want to come out here for?"

"I don't know. Get away from my family, I guess."

"They say anything about it?"

I shrugged.

She propped her elbows on the table and leaned toward me, her blond hair swinging over her cheeks.

"You know what my mother did when I got ready to move down to the Cities? She called my sister and told her, 'I don't want Marlene going out at night unless you're with her.' You like that? She calls Minneapolis 'Sin City.' She'd shit if I moved to New York."

We laughed, Marlene's laugh a quick snort of air, mine a little too loud. Whatever was going to be told about New York at that table was going to be told by me, and the feeling that went with knowing that was like the rush of warmth that runs through you toward the end of your first beer.

"Could I ask you something?" Marlene said.

I waited, smiling my agreement.

"Were you baptized Jewish?"

I watched the smoke rise from her cigarette while I turned the question over, trying to figure out what was strange about it. It seemed so natural, the way she asked it.

"Jews don't get baptized," I said finally.

"Why not?"

"Well, that's a Christian thing."

She scraped the coal of her cigarette against the ashtray. "So?"

"So Jews aren't Christians."

"Why not?"

"Because they're Jews."

Somewhere in my head the word *they* registered the way *baptised* had—something was odd about it, but I didn't have time to sort it out.

"Don't you believe in Jesus?"

"That he lived. Not that he was holy."

"You don't believe that he died on the cross for you?"

I thought of the billboard outside my window, where Christ died every morning with my coffee.

"I believe he died on a cross."

"I thought Jews were Christians." She drew on the cigarette and scraped the coal clean again. "I mean, everybody's Lutheran where I grew up. I heard about Jews, but I thought they were just some other Protestant and I couldn't figure out why nobody liked them."

We let our eyes go into long focus and looked past each other. Marlene smoked. I brought the coffee pot over and poured us each another cup.

"You're sure you're not Christian?"

"I'm sure."

"Don't you believe in God?"

"My parents do."

"But you don't believe in Christ our Lord?"

I shook my head, sat at the end of the booth and waited, the coffeepot on the table between us.

"That's terrible. I'll always think of that when I see a Jewish person." But even this she said without anger, as if it had to do only with the idea of Jews, not with me, and so I felt nothing beyond the surprise that any town in Wisconsin could be so small, so completely Lutheran.

***

That afternoon the temperature dropped below anything I'd understood to be possible, and on the way home from work the windshield of my VW frosted over inside as fast as I could scrape it clear. I left the radio on all evening for the weather reports, drinking beer and listening as the mercury slid from zero to fifteen below.

Somewhere into my third beer, I moved from the couch to the kitchen table, wedged myself into the chair and stared across the parking lot at the white cloth draped around Jesus' hips. He was lit by floodlights that made him whiter than he looked in the daylight. The wind had picked up and was blowing knife-thin streams of snow off the edges of the drifts. *Was it nothing to me*, hell. Was it nothing to *them?* I opened my fourth beer and found half a piece of chicken in the refrigerator, and I brought them back to the table so I could keep the poor bastard company. I worked out a program for the church to take that responsibility: They'd build a shelter in the parking lot, where two church members at a time would sit with the old boy. They probably shouldn't eat while they were on duty, but a drink or two would be appropriate. I lifted my beer to him and drank.

At this point I was struck by the revelation that the way not to hesitate was to act. I'd been in the Midwest long enough to stop thinking so much. I abandoned my beer, hauled my jacket out of the closet and pulled money from my purse and from the bottom of my underwear drawer, distributing it randomly in my pockets—quarters, pennies, paper money mashed small and flat as if it were all so much kleenex.

The hardware store was empty when I got there, all bare wooden floors and a smell like Sunday afternoon dust. I brought my can of spray paint to the register and counted money out of one pocket after another until I had the exact change, which I seemed to believe would keep the clerk from looking into my face to read either my intentions or my nationality.

As the door closed behind me, the clerk flipped the *open* sign to *closed*. The window lights went dark as I crossed the street, and the wind howled down my collar straight out of Canada. The cowboy drew his lasso tight around the steer's neck, then tightened it all over again. I wrapped my scarf over my chin and nose, stumbling up the barricade of snow at the rim of the church parking lot, sinking knee-deep at the top, then staggering out on the other side with snow in my shoes and the spray can tucked warm into my armpit.

From the hood of a parked car, I climbed to the catwalk below the billboard, and standing on my toes, with one glove stuffed into my pocket and my fingers as cold as Jesus' blue-white feet, I painted boots and leggings that reached to his knees. Then, beside him in sprawling letters, I wrote, *Buy the poor schmuck a coat.*

I jumped down from the catwalk elated, but as I crossed the parking lot the feeling drained out of me.

"Foolishness," my father's voice whispered in my head. "For this you should put yourself in danger?"

I told us both that there was no danger, and having put words to the thought I looked around to make sure I was right. The street was deserted. The air was so cold that every time I breathed in, the hairs inside my nostrils froze. When I got back to my apartment, the heat was overwhelming, and I opened the window behind the couch, letting the air flow over my face and neck. I thought about my father's voice and how it must have lain coiled inside my head all this time, waiting to whisper caution. I shook my head to clear him away and read the warnings on the paint can: Use in a well-ventilated area. I cleared a space on my landlord's kitchen table and spray-painted a star of David.

From his billboard, Jesus watched without approving or disapproving. He wore completely unrecognizable boots and leggings. I looked from him to the table and found no comfort in either place. I was as heavy as if two thousand years of Jewish history had just descended on me—the diaspora, the burning of Jews and synagogues during the plague, the small Lutheran towns where no one liked Jews and no one remembered why. Outside, the nails in Jesus' hands and feet drew the cold down into his bones.

I wedged myself into my chair at the kitchen table, breathing the sharp, insufficiently ventilated smell of paint, and picked up the almost empty beer that I'd left when I went out. I set it down in the center of the star of David, then moved it outside the star, then inside again, then out, so it became Jew and not-Jew, Jew and not-Jew. That easily. Each time I put it down I meant to leave it, but each time I picked it back up and moved it, until finally I drank the last flat swallow and stood up, setting it down on the edge of the star. And there I was able to let it rest, in that narrow zone where the paint became sparse, where star faded into not-star, where the words wouldn't bind us.

CONTRIBUTORS' NOTES

Marianne Barnett writes to us from Saginaw, Michigan. **Julia Crozier,** co-owner and operator of Big River Studio and Gallery in Bellevue, Iowa, concentrates on realistic pen and ink drawings, natural landscape watercolors, and design work using symbols from ancient cultures. **Deborah Cummins,** Evanston, Illinois, has had work appear in *New England Review, Whetstone, Other Voices,* and elsewhere. **Florence Dacey's** biographical note is on page 69. **Robert Edwards,** St. Paul, has had work published in several literary magazines, including previously in *Great River Review.* He has published two collections: *Radio Vinceremos* and *Nixies.* **Mitch Grabois** is a regular columnist for Solares Hill, Key West's weekly, alternative newspaper, and has published numerous short stories in literary and commercial periodicals. **Tom Hansen** teaches at Northern State U. in Aberdeen, South Dakota. Recent work of his has appeared in *College English, North Dakota Review, The Iowa Review,* and elsewhere. **L. L. Harper** resides in South Carolina and has had work in *The Georgia Review, The Massachusetts Review, Passages North,* and elsewhere. **Ellen Hawley,** St. Paul, is editor of *The View from the Loft.* Her work is included in the anthology, *26 Minnesota Writers.* **Jeanne Lyon** is completing a Master's degree in religious studies. "Looking for a Heart" is her first published poem. **Jim Murphy** is in the Master's program at the University of Cincinnati. He has published poetry previously in *Midlands, Chants,* and *Puerto del Sol.* **Howard Nelson** writes us from Moravia, New York. **John Reinhard's** biographical note is on page 15. **Linda Goodman Robiner** teaches at Notre Dame College of Ohio and has published her poetry and fiction in numerous journals, including *Chiron Review* and *Black River Review.* **Matthew J. Spireng** has had work appear in numerous literary magazines, including formerly in *Great River Review.* He is the assistant city editor of the Kingston (N.Y.) *Daily Freeman.* **Scott Wrobel,** from the Creative Writing Program at Southwest State University in Marshall, Minnesota, now writes us from Spokane, Washington.